MINI MAKERS

by Rebecca Felix and
Ruthie Van Oosbree

CAPSTONE PRESS
a capstone imprint

Dabble Lab is published by Capstone Press, an imprint of Capstone.
1710 Roe Crest Drive, North Mankato, Minnesota 56003
capstonepub.com

Copyright © 2024 by Capstone. All rights reserved. No part of this publication may be reproduced in whole or in part, or stored in a retrieval system, or transmitted in any form or by any means, electronic, mechanical, photocopying, recording, or otherwise, without written permission of the publisher.

Library of Congress Cataloging-in-Publication Data is available on the Library of Congress website.
ISBN: 9781669016618 (hardcover)
ISBN: 9781669016588 (ebook PDF)

Summary: Looking to host a game night? Think mini! Craft a bitty bowling alley for marble bowling balls. Create a deck of petite playing cards. Construct little darts for a magnetic mini dartboard. Then play your games with family and friends. Tiny games are tons of fun!

Image Credits
iStockphoto: avean (font), Front Cover, 1, Back Cover; Mighty Media, Inc.: project photos; Shutterstock: donatas1205, 5 (right), Feng Yu, 5 (left), TabitaZn, Back Cover (gift tag)

Design Elements
iStockphoto: Tolga TEZCAN; Shutterstock: ds_vector, Valerii_M

Editorial Credits
Editor: Jessica Rusick
Designers: Aruna Rangarajan, Sarah DeYoung

All internet sites appearing in back matter were available and accurate when this book was sent to press.

The publisher and the author shall not be liable for any damages allegedly arising from the information in this book, and they specifically disclaim any liability from the use or application of any of the contents of this book.

TABLE OF CONTENTS

Mini Games 4

Mini Word Game 6

Mini Checkers 8

Mini Bowling 10

Mini Deck of Cards 12

Mini Dominoes 14

Mini Peg Solitaire 16

Mini Stick and Marble Game 18

Mini Ladder Ball 20

Mini Four-in-a-Row 24

Mini Magnetic Darts 28

Read More 32

Internet Sites 32

About the Authors 32

MINI GAMES

Board games, cards, and games of skill are tons of fun to play with friends and family. But what if these games were small enough to fit in your pocket? The projects in this book will let you bring fun games with you wherever you go!

Play solitaire any time with a **super-small deck of cards.**

Hang a **tiny magnetic dart board** on a refrigerator or locker.

Or challenge your friends to a **little game of ladder ball.**

Whatever you choose, these mini games will be a blast to **MAKE** and **PLAY!**

BASIC SUPPLIES

- » beads
- » buttons
- » card stock
- » hot glue gun
- » markers
- » paints and paintbrushes
- » pipe cleaners
- » ruler
- » scissors
- » string

Crafting Tips

SET YOURSELF UP FOR SUCCESS! Read through the materials and instructions before starting a project. Cover your workspace with paper or plastic to protect it from messes or spills.

LET YOUR CREATIVITY SHINE! Put your own stamp on these projects. Don't be afraid to make changes or try something new!

UPCYCLE! Lots of the projects in this book use materials you'll likely find around your home. Is there something you can't find? Think of ways to adapt the project using items you do have.

ASK FIRST! Get permission to do the projects and to use any materials you find at home or school.

SAFETY FIRST! Ask an adult for help with projects that require sharp or hot tools.

CLEAN UP! When you're finished crafting, make sure to put away any supplies you took out. Clean up any spills and wipe down your crafting surface.

5

Mini WORD GAME

Use small magazine letters to build words on a teeny game board!

MATERIALS

- » old magazines
- » scissors
- » ¼-inch (0.6-centimeter) buttons
- » craft glue
- » tweezers or craft stick (optional)
- » checkered paper with ¼-inch (0.6-cm) squares
- » cardboard
- » construction paper
- » small bag

1

Cut out at least 50 capital letters from old magazines. Include at least one of each letter in the alphabet. Also cut out duplicates of common letters. These include A, D, E, G, I, L, N, O, R, S, and T. The letters can vary in size, but each letter must be small enough to fit on one button.

2

Glue each letter to a button. Use tweezers or a craft stick to place the letters if needed.

3

Cut the checkered paper so it is 10 squares long on each side.

4

Cut a piece of cardboard the same size as the checkered paper. Glue the checkered paper on top of the cardboard.

5

Cut a 6-by-2-inch (15-by-5-cm) strip of construction paper. Fold the strip in half lengthwise. Unfold the strip. Fold one long side up to meet the center crease. This is the letter tray. Repeat to make a second letter tray.

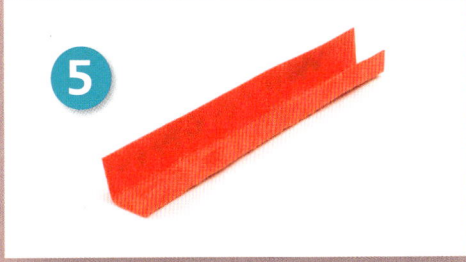

6

Place the letters in the small bag. You're ready for a game!

HOW TO PLAY

Each player draws seven letters from the bag and arranges them on their letter tray. Take turns making words on the board, placing one button per square. Any new word must build off a previous word on the board, using one letter from that word. After each turn, a player draws replacement letters. Each word that is two to four letters long is worth one point. Words that are five or more letters are worth two points. **The first player to reach 15 points wins!**

Mini CHECKERS

Use hook-and-loop tape to keep a tiny game of checkers intact on the go!

MATERIALS

- » cardboard
- » pencil
- » ruler
- » scissors
- » hook-and-loop tape (scratchy and soft)
- » paints (2 colors) and paintbrushes
- » painter's tape
- » ¼-inch (0.6-cm) buttons in 2 colors (12 of each color)

1
Draw a 4-by-4-inch (10-by-10-cm) square on cardboard and cut it out.

2
Cover the square in strips of scratchy hook-and-loop tape. Paint the tape in one color and let it dry.

3
Cut eight strips of painter's tape 4 inches (10 cm) long by ½ inch (1.3 cm) wide.

4
Place one painter's tape strip along an edge of the square. Place three more strips on the square so they are ½ inch (1.3 cm) apart from each other. Repeat with the four remaining strips of tape, placing them perpendicular to the first set.

5

Paint the hook-and-loop squares showing through the grid in a second color. Dab on the paint instead of brushing to create clean lines. Let the paint dry.

6

Lift the tape grid in one piece and rotate it 180 degrees. Repeat step 5 to paint any newly showing squares. Then remove the grid.

7

Cut 24 circles of soft hook-and-loop tape to the size of the buttons. Tape each circle to the bottom of a button.

8

Your checkerboard and checkers are complete. Challenge a friend or family member to a game!

Mini BOWLING

Build a little bowling lane and knock down petite bowling pins!

MATERIALS

- » mat board
- » craft knife
- » ruler
- » 4 straws
- » glue
- » standard washi tape
- » scissors
- » narrow washi tape
- » 10 caps from old, dried out markers
- » marble

1
Use the craft knife to cut a 3-by-16-inch (8-by-41-cm) piece of mat board. This will be the bowling lane.

2
Glue two straws to each long side of the lane to create bumpers.

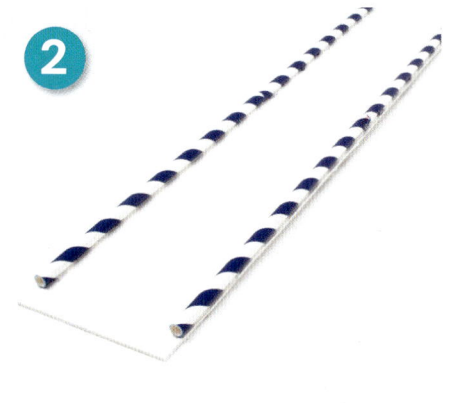

3
Cut 10 small squares of standard washi tape. Place them at one end of the lane in rows of four, three, two, and one. These mark where the bowling pins will stand.

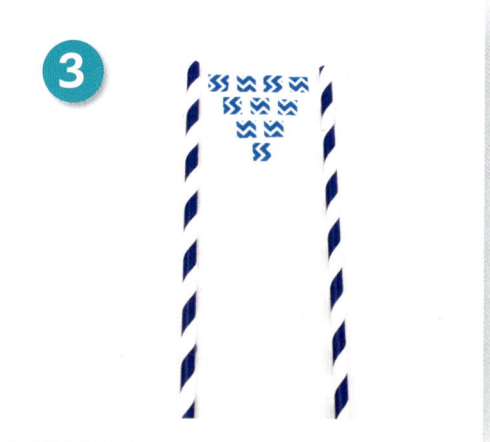

4

Wrap a strip of narrow washi tape around each marker cap near one end. These are the pins' stripes.

5

Set up the pins on the tape squares. You're ready to bowl! Roll the marble toward the pins from the opposite end of the lane. How many pins can you topple?

11

Mini DECK OF CARDS

> **MATERIALS**
>
> » 2 sheets patterned card stock (white on one side)
> » pencil
> » ruler
> » scissors
> » 1 sheet plain card stock
> » washable markers in 2 colors
> » matchbox
> » tape

Keep this itty-bitty box in your pocket to play card games anywhere!

1

Draw vertical lines on the white side of one patterned card stock sheet. Space the lines 1 inch (2.5 cm) apart.

2

Draw horizontal lines across the card stock sheet, each 1½ inches (4 cm) apart. This will create a grid of rectangles. Each rectangle will be a card.

3

Draw each suit (clubs, diamonds, hearts, and spades) on the plain card stock sheet. Cut out the shapes. The card stock is now a stencil.

4

Use the stencil and markers to create 13 cards of each suit on the card stock grid. Draw the suit in the middle of the card. Make the spades and clubs one color and the diamonds and hearts another color.

5

Draw the letter or number of each card in two opposite corners of each rectangle. Each suit should have one of each card: A, 2, 3, 4, 5, 6, 7, 8, 9, 10, J, Q, K. Cut out the cards.

6

Cut a strip of card stock from the second patterned sheet. Make it as long as the matchbox and several times its width. Wrap the strip around the matchbox cover and tape it in place. The matchbox will store the cards.

7

Your deck of cards is complete! Play solitaire or pack up the cards to use later with more players.

13

Mini DOMINOES

MATERIALS
- » ¼ inch (0.6 cm) wide balsa wood sticks
- » ruler
- » pencil
- » craft knife
- » sandpaper
- » painter's tape
- » paints and paintbrushes
- » fine-tip permanent marker

These tiny wood dominoes will be a hit at any game night!

1
Use the pencil to mark ½-inch (1.3-cm) sections along a balsa wood stick. Repeat on more sticks to make 28 sections total.

2
Using the craft knife, cut the balsa wood sticks at each pencil mark.

3
Tape a piece of sandpaper to a flat surface. Sand the ends of each balsa wood piece to make them square and smooth.

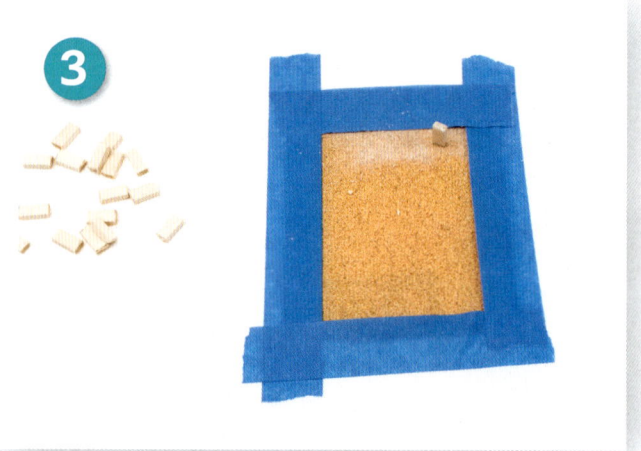

4
Paint the pieces and let them dry. Use as many colors as you want.

14

5

Use the fine-tip permanent marker to draw a line down the center of each piece. Draw dots on either side of the line. These dots are called pips. A domino with one pip on one half and two pips on the other is a 1-2 domino. Dominoes with the same number of pips on one half make up a suit. For example, dominoes that all have one pip on one half are the suit of one. To make a double-six set, label the dominoes with these pips:

suit of zero: 0-0, 0-1, 0-2, 0-3, 0-4, 0-5, 0-6
suit of one: 1-1, 1-2, 1-3, 1-4, 1-5, 1-6
suit of two: 2-2, 2-3, 2-4, 2-5, 2-6
suit of three: 3-3, 3-4, 3-5, 3-6
suit of four: 4-4, 4-5, 4-6
suit of five: 5-5, 5-6
suit of six: 6-6

6

You're ready to play any double-six set game of dominoes!

Mini PEG SOLITAIRE

MATERIALS
- » air-dry clay
- » butter knife
- » ruler
- » 14 pin nails
- » paints and paintbrushes

Create a colorful tricky triangle game from clay and tiny nails!

1

Use the butter knife to form air-dry clay into a small triangle with sides 2 inches (4 cm) long. Press the front and back sides of the triangle onto a hard surface to flatten them.

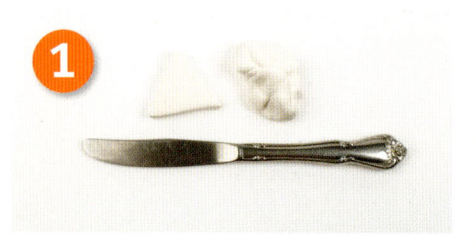

2

Poke holes into the triangle using the pin nail. Assign one corner as the top and make one hole there. Then make rows of two, three, four, and five holes. Wiggle the nail slightly in each hole to widen it. This will help the nails fit in with ease once the clay is dry.

3

Let the clay dry overnight. Then paint the triangle. Use many colors or try fun designs if you'd like! Let the paint dry.

4

Paint the nails and let them dry.

5

You're ready to play! Place the nails in the triangle, leaving one corner hole empty. Choose a starting nail and jump over the others one at a time into an empty hole. Remove each jumped nail. The game's goal is to end with one nail left on the board!

TINY TIP

Use a stiff paintbrush to create a splatter effect! Dip the brush in paint and use your fingers to flick paint from its tip.

Mini STICK AND MARBLE GAME

MATERIALS

- » capped plastic bottle about 3 inches (7.6 cm) tall
- » nail
- » mini dowels
- » scissors
- » small jar lid
- » decorative tape
- » hot glue gun
- » craft knife
- » beads

Use mini dowels and beads to create this fun and challenging game!

1

Use the nail to poke a hole anywhere in the top third of the bottle. Poke a second hole opposite the first. Repeat to make 12 pairs of holes.

2

Cut 12 mini dowels to be about twice as long as the diameter of the bottle.

3

Insert a dowel piece into one hole, across the bottle, and out the other hole. Repeat with the remaining dowel pieces.

4

Decorate the bottle cap and jar lid with tape.

18

5

Glue the bottom of the bottle to the top of the jar lid.

6

Use the craft knife to cut two windows into opposite sides of the bottle near the bottom. The windows allow you to remove fallen beads during gameplay.

7

Remove the bottle cap and fill the bottle with beads. They should rest on the dowels. Put the bottle cap back on the bottle.

8

You're ready to play! Take turns with another player pulling the dowels out one a time. Try not to let the beads drop. Whoever drops the fewest beads wins!

Mini LADDER BALL

Create paper clip ladders and land bead bolas on them!

MATERIALS

- » 12 large paper clips
- » washi tape (2 colors optional)
- » scissors
- » ruler
- » pipe cleaners
- » string in 2 colors
- » pencil
- » 12 large beads in 2 colors (6 of each)

1

Unwind a paper clip into a partial rectangle. Repeat with a second paper clip.

2

Fit the unwound paper clips together to make a rectangle. Overlap the arms of the paper clips on two sides. Wrap the overlapped areas in washi tape to hold them together. These will be the vertical sides of the ladder.

3

Hold the paper clip rectangle upright. Clip four paper clips along its bottom side to build a base. Make sure each paper clip's smaller loop faces up. Alternate the direction the open end of each paper clip faces. The base should hold the rectangle upright.

4

Cover the base paper clips in washi tape to hold them in place.

5

Cut two 3-inch (8-cm) pipe cleaner pieces. Wrap the ends of each piece around the rectangle to make horizontal bars. Space the bars about equal distance from the top and bottom and from one another. Trim any excess pipe cleaner ends.

6

Repeat steps 1 through 5 to make a second ladder. Use different colored washi tape if you'd like.

CONTINUED ON THE NEXT PAGE »

7

Cut six 4-inch (10-cm) pieces of string.

8

Measure 1½ inches (4 cm) in from one end of a string piece. Mark the spot with a pencil.

9

Tie a knot at the marked spot on the string. Then thread a bead onto the string. The knot should keep the bead from falling off.

10

Thread a second matching bead onto the string. Then measure 1½ inches (4 cm) in from the string's unknotted end. Mark this spot and tie a knot there.

11

Cut the excess string off both ends. Then slide the beads so one is at each end of the string. This game piece is called a bola.

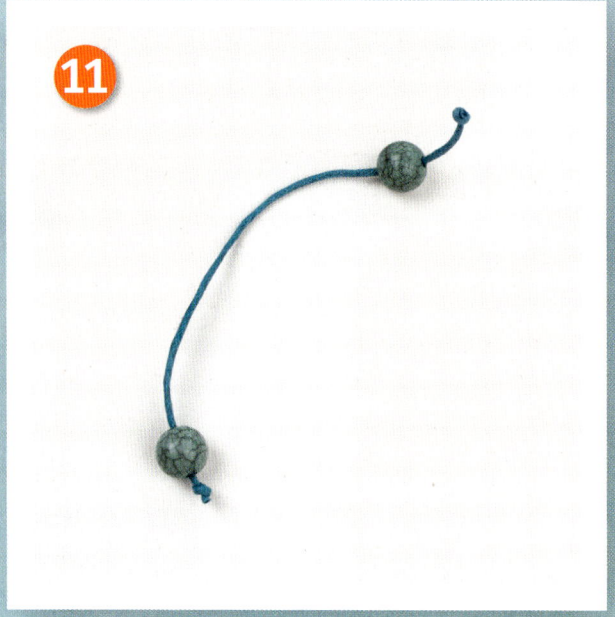

TINY TIP
If the bead falls off the string, tie a double knot instead of a single knot.

12

Repeat steps 8 through 11 to create six bolas total.

13

You're ready to play ladder ball! Grab a second player and set up the ladders to play together.

HOW TO PLAY

Each player gets three matching bolas. Take turns tossing them on the ladders. Landing on the top rung is worth three points. The second rung is two points. The lowest rung is one point. **The first player to reach 10 points without going over wins!**

Mini FOUR-IN-A-ROW

Turn a matchbox into a gameboard. Take turns trying to connect four game pieces in a row!

MATERIALS

- » matchbox
- » scissors
- » ruler
- » pencil
- » ¼-inch (0.6 cm) hole punch
- » paint and paintbrush
- » hot glue gun
- » pipe cleaners in 2 colors

1

Remove the matchbox's cover. Cut it along the long edges to make two equal-sized pieces.

2

Draw a 4-by-6 grid of squares on the inside of one cover piece. The squares' sides should be about ¼ inch (0.6 cm) long.

3

Stack the cover pieces on top of each other with the grid facing up. Make sure the pieces line up.

24

4

Use the grid as a guide to punch holes through both pieces. Punch the holes in the center of each square. Make sure the holes don't overlap one another or the edges of the matchbox halves.

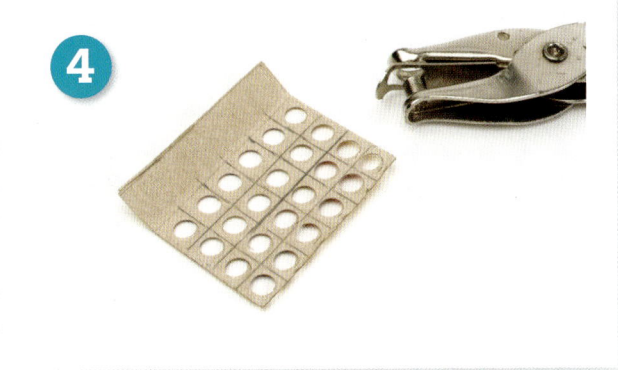

5

Paint the punched matchbox halves and the matchbox tray. Let the paint dry.

6

Fold the punched pieces back into a box shape. Glue the cut edges back together.

CONTINUED ON THE NEXT PAGE »

25

7

Turn the matchbox tray upside down. Stand the punched matchbox cover on the tray. Glue it in place.

8

Cut 12 pieces of pipe cleaner in one color. Make each one ¾ inch (1.9 cm) long. Cut 12 more pieces in the other pipe cleaner color. These 24 stems are the game pieces.

9

Challenge a friend to a game of four-in-a-row!

HOW TO PLAY

Have each player choose a game piece color. Take turns placing one game piece at a time in the game board. **Whoever first makes a chain of four pieces wins!** A row of four can run vertically, horizontally, or diagonally.

26

TINY TIP
When you're ready to put the game away, store the game pieces by poking them through the game board.

Mini MAGNETIC DARTS

MATERIALS
- » sheet magnet
- » 1 tin can
- » paint markers
- » scissors
- » 3 objects (each smaller than the last) with round bottoms smaller than the tin can
- » ruler
- » 3 mini dowels
- » 6 button magnets
- » tacky glue
- » washi tape

Make miniscule darts to launch at a small magnetic dartboard!

1
Trace the bottom of the tin can on the sheet magnet. Cut the circle out.

2
Center the second-largest object inside the cutout circle and trace the object. Repeat with the third-largest object and the smallest object.

3
Color in the smallest circle. Make a small dot in the center of the circle. This is the dartboard's bull's-eye.

4
Place the ruler diagonally through the dartboard's bull's-eye. Draw a diagonal line through the dartboard's three inner circles.

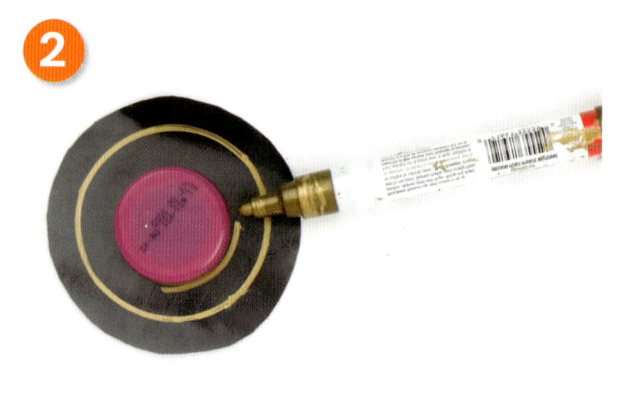

5

Draw a second diagonal line through the dartboard's three inner circles that forms an X with the first diagonal line. Draw a horizontal line that passes through the X's center.

6

There are now three lines through the center of the bull's-eye. Widen each half of each line into a wedge shape. The narrow part of the wedge should be near the bull's-eye. The dartboard's three inner circles should now be divided into 12 slices. Trace the circle outlines in different colors for decoration if you'd like.

CONTINUED ON THE NEXT PAGE »

7
Cut three mini dowels in half to make six darts.

8
Paint three darts in one color. Paint the other darts in a second color.

9
Glue a button magnet onto one end of each dart.

10
Wrap each dart end opposite the magnet in washi tape. Cut the tape edges into angles or fringe. This is the dart's fletching. It helps the dart fly straight.

TINY TIP
Weak button magnets work best for darts. These magnets will not stick together if the darts land near each other on the dartboard!

11

Stick your dartboard to a magnetic surface, such as a refrigerator. Then grab a friend for a match!

HOW TO PLAY

Take turns throwing the mini darts at the dartboard. Landing a dart in the outer ring is worth one point. The next rings in are worth two points, three points, and four points. Hitting the bull's-eye is worth five points!

READ MORE

The Highlights Book of Things to Do: Discover, Explore, Create, and Do Great Things. Honesdale, PA: Highlights for Children, Inc., 2020.

Kukla, Lauren. *Mini Machines that Zoom and Spin.* North Mankato, MN: Capstone Press, 2023.

Seed, Andy. *The Anti-Boredom Book of Brilliant Things to Do: Games, Crafts, Puzzles, Jokes, Riddles, and Trivia for Hours of Fun.* New York: Skyhorse Publishing, 2020.

INTERNET SITES

Funbrain: Games, Videos, and Books for Kids
funbrain.com

75 Fun Indoor Games for Kids
familyfuntwincities.com/indoor-games-for-kids/

30 Classic Outdoor Games for Kids
wired.com/2009/08/simpleoutdoorplay/

ABOUT THE AUTHORS

Rebecca Felix is an author and editor of children's books. She loves brainstorming crafts, taking hikes, camping, and learning about all kinds of topics! She collects houseplants in her Minnesota home, where she lives with her funny husband, joyful daughter, and sleepy dog.

Ruthie Van Oosbree is a writer and editor who loves making crafts. In her free time, she enjoys doing word puzzles, reading, and playing the piano. She lives with her husband and three cats in the Twin Cities.